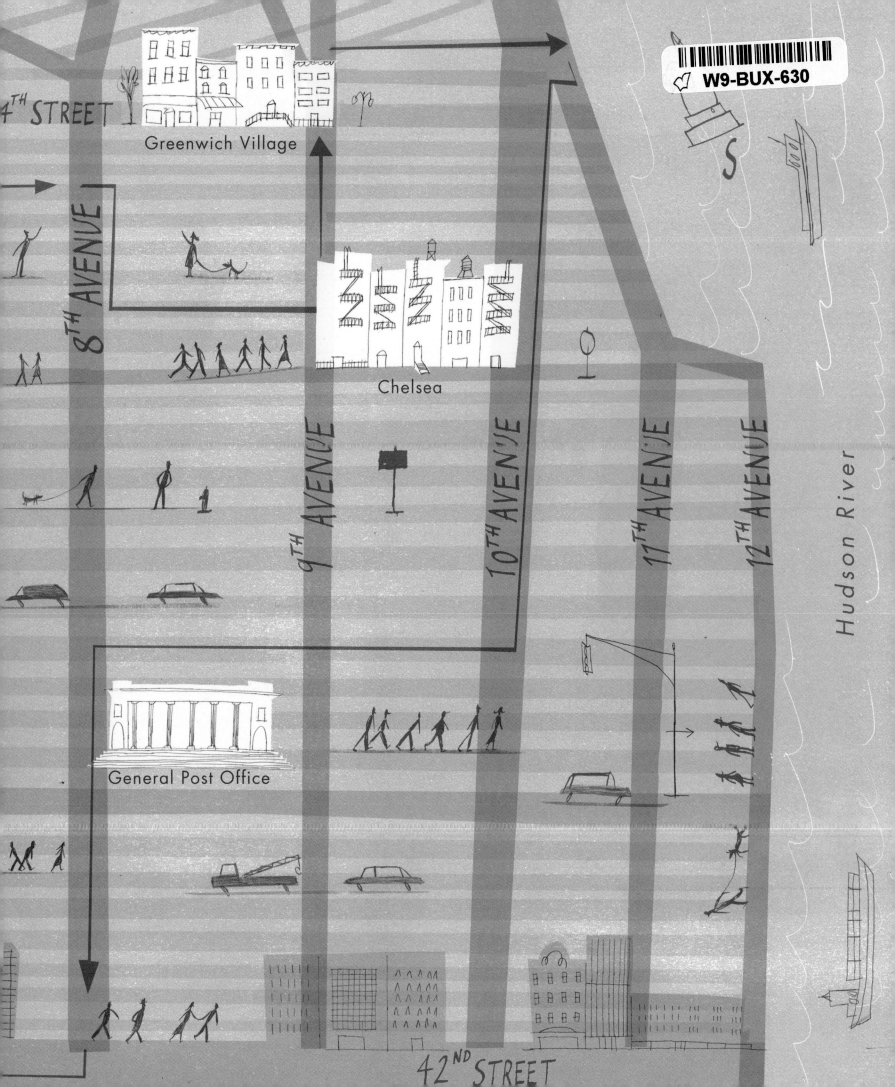

First U.S. edition 2009

Library of Congress Cataloging-in-Publication Data

Rubbino, Salvatore, date.
A Walk in New York / Salvatore Rubbino. —1st U.S. ed.
p. —cm.
ISBN 978-0-7636-3855-9
1. New York (N.Y.)—Description and travel—Juvenile literature.
2. Historic buildings—New York (State)—New York—Juvenile literature.
3. New York (N.Y.)—Buildings, structures, etc.—Juvenile literature.
4. Walking—New York (State)—New York—Juvenile literature. I. Title.
F128.33.R83—2009
917.47'10444—dc22—2008020787

09 10 11 12 13 14 CCP 10 9 8 7 6 5 4 3

Printed in Shenzhen, Guangdong, China

This book was typeset in MKlang Bold and Futura Book.
The illustrations were done in mixed media.

Candlewick Press
99 Dover Street
Somerville, Massachusetts 02144

visit us at www.candlewick.com

For **HAIDEE**
who waited for me
to come home

special thanks
to
LUCY
&
BETH

These trains have all arrived from the north.

A WALK IN NEW YORK

SALVATORE RUBBINO

CANDLEWICK PRESS

and come up onto ground level.
"Welcome to **GRAND CENTRAL**,"
Dad says. "The largest train station
in the world!"

WOW! This hall is really huge.
And there are so many people—
all in a hurry.

TRACK 32

TRACK 31

Grand Central Terminal
has more platforms (44)
and more tracks (67) than
any other railway station in the world.

8

Hello! This is **me**, and that's my dad! We've just arrived in Manhattan— the busiest part of **New York City!** Dad wants to show me around.

This platform's underground. We walk along a ramp . . .

New Yorkers call
the three main areas
of Manhattan
uptown,
midtown,
and downtown.

This is midtown, where
more people work than live.

GRAND CENTRAL TERMINAL

U.S MAIL

10

The clock in the middle of Grand Central Terminal has four sides, so you can see the time wherever you are.

The ceiling shows 2,500 stars in a night sky and the constellations of the zodiac.

INFORMATION

TICKETS

About 125,000 people travel to and from Grand Central Terminal every day.

9

We step out onto the street, and I can't believe my eyes! The buildings are so TALL; no wonder they're called skyscrapers.

I can tell who the visitors are:

we're the ones who keep stopping to look up!

Sailors used to call the sails at the top of ship masts skyscrapers.

11

We stop again. This building's not as tall as it is WIDE.
Dad tells me it's the NEW YORK PUBLIC LIBRARY.
"And meet the library lions!" he says. "They guard the books inside."
Dad's silly—those lions aren't alive!

The New York Public Library opened in 1911 with a collection
of more than one million books, including children's books.

NEW YORK

The library lions are called
Patience and Fortitude.
They're made of pink marble
from Tennessee.

A librarian stops to talk to us. She says 10,000 new books come in every week, and there are 88 miles of bookshelves inside!

PUBLIC LIBRARY

The site where the library stands used to be a reservoir.

TAXI →

I recognize that skyscraper! It's the
Empire State Building.

"It has a hundred and two
floors," Dad says.
"On cloudy days you
can't see the top!"

The Empire
State Building
isn't the
tallest building
in the world—
but it is one
of them!

NOW
OPEN

ICE COLD
DRINKS

PIZZA

NY NAILS

Deli

LEE 212
FUNG $4
3¢

HOTEL
★★★

14

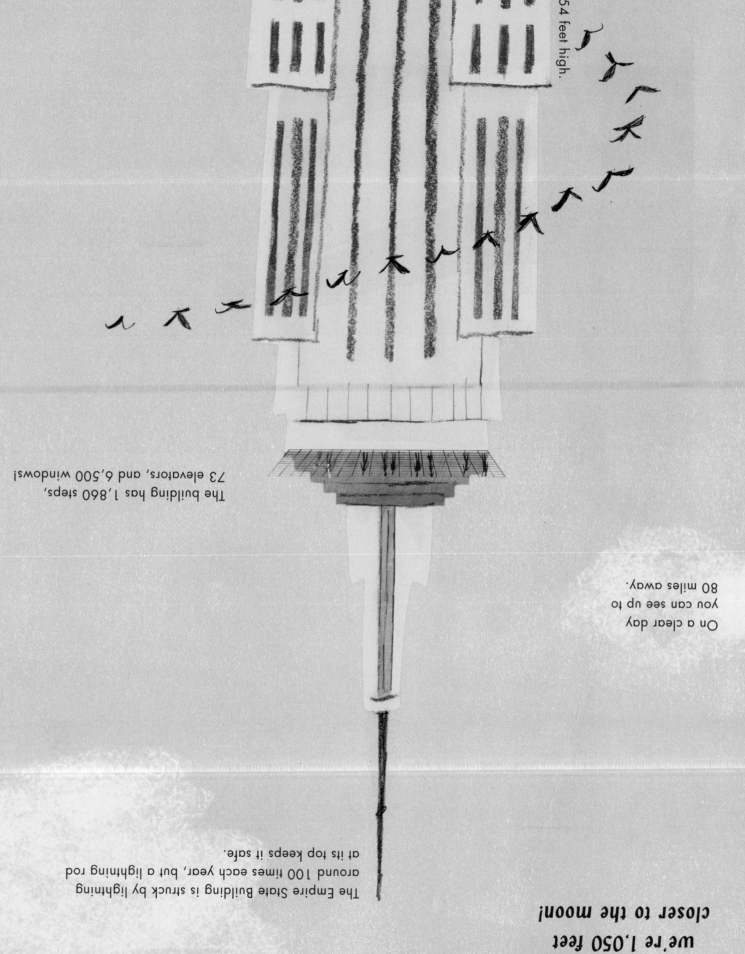

ds 1,454 feet high.

The building has 1,860 steps,
73 elevators, and 6,500 windows!

On a clear day
you can see up to
80 miles away.

The Empire State Building is struck by lightning
around 100 times each year, but a lightning rod
at its top keeps it safe.

and in less than a minute,
we're 1,050 feet
closer to the moon!

Visitors can go up the Empire State Building, so Dad and I
buy tickets. A policeman shows us to a high-speed elevator . . .

The Empire State Building has an observatory on the 86th floor. It's open every single day of the year.

Lift page here

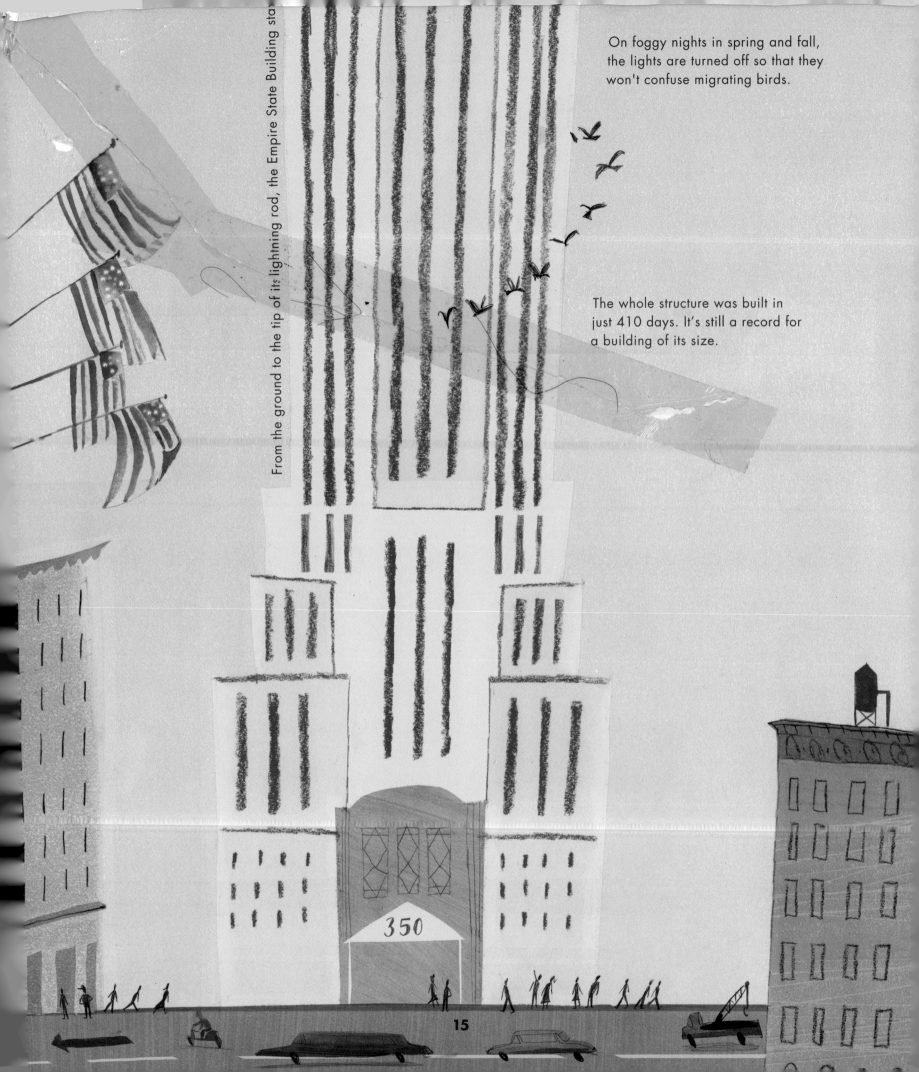

On foggy nights in spring and fall, the lights are turned off so that they won't confuse migrating birds.

From the ground to the tip of its lightning rod, the Empire State Building sta

The whole structure was built in just 410 days. It's still a record for a building of its size.

350

It's quiet up here, and water shines in all directions.
Dad tells me that Manhattan is an island.
He shows me some bridges that connect it
to New York's other boroughs.

BROOKLYN BRIDGE

MANHATTAN BRIDGE

WILLIAMSBURG
BRIDGE

New York City is made
up of five "boroughs"
or counties—the Bronx,
Brooklyn, Manhattan,
Queens, and Staten Island.

I look down, and the cars are tiny specks
in the ribbon streets below.

This view faces south
to New York Bay and
the Atlantic Ocean.

17

Back on Planet Earth, we smell a DELICIOUS smell!
But to get to the hot-dog stand, we have to cross
the street! Five lanes of traffic are revving
at the lights. Dad puts me on his shoulders.
I think he thinks that I'll be safer there.

More hot dogs are eaten in New York
than anywhere else in the U.S.

macy's

Macy's is one of the oldest stores in New York. It opened in 1858.

R.H.MACY & CO.

YAP!

Yum!

Only dogs you can carry (not including hot dogs!) are allowed inside a Macy's store.

We eat our hot dogs and window-shop. This department store is called Macy's. Dad says that you can buy anything from a dishrag to a diamond inside.

NYC

Macy's was one of the first stores to have big window displays.

What did you get?

That must be why their shopping bags come in so many shapes and sizes!

Now we're walking down a street called **BROADWAY**. Dad shows me an amazing skyscraper—it isn't square-shaped; it's triangular! "It's called the **Flatiron Building**," Dad says, "because it looks just like an iron."

Broadway is New York's oldest and longest street. Its American Indian name is the Wickquasgeck Trail.

The Flatiron Building is one of New York's oldest sky-scrapers. It has 22 floors.

Most Manhattan streets run straight, but Broadway runs *diagonally.*

23

The greenmarket in Union Square Park
sells local farmers' fresh fruit and vegetables.

UNION SQUARE

My feet are really tired—even Dad's are—so we find
a park to rest in. It's called UNION SQUARE PARK.
We buy some fruit and postcards at a market stall,
then sit down in the grass and listen to the music.

24

This statue in Union Square Park of George Washington on his horse is made of bronze. It's the oldest sculpture in all the New York City parks.

After our energy comes back, we want to see some more! The streets around the park are quieter and smaller.

Dad says the buildings here are mainly homes, not offices. People know one another, and when they talk, we hear lots of different languages.

Most people in Manhattan live in apartments.

Around 170 different languages are spoken in New York.

DON'T HONK $350 PENALTY

Ciao!

Preevyet!

Ahn nyeong!

Hola!

— Ni hao!

Many old apartment buildings have iron stairways down the outside walls in case of fire and water towers on the roof.

More people live in New York than in any other city in the U.S.

Marhabah!

Salut!

TAXI

The ground under Greenwich Village is too soft to build skyscrapers on.

Most Manhattan streets are known by their numbers, but the streets in Greenwich Village usually have names.

The Village used to be a real village that was outside New York City.

VILLAGE CAFE

271

The more we walk now, the more we see the sky!

Dad asks me if I'm hungry. I always am!
"Let's have a snack," he says.
"This is **Greenwich Village**,
where you find the best cafés in New York!"

29

We leave the café when it's almost dark.
Dad slips down a side street that brings us to the river.
"The Hudson!" he says. "And can you see the STATUE OF LIBERTY?"

From the pier, we watch the boats. The gulls watch us,
and the fishermen watch the water. The sun dips
behind the statue and
turns her crown
to gold.

About 200
different kinds
of fish live in the
Hudson River.

The statue's crown has seven rays because the world has seven seas and seven continents.

The statue is more than 300 feet high and was given to New York by the people of France in 1886.

The statue is green because it's made out of copper, which doesn't stay red unless you polish it.

Manhattan is a port. Oil, molasses, cocoa beans, grain, machinery, and lots of other things pass up and down the river in ships and tanker barges.

The Hudson is a tidal river, and its American Indian name is Muhheakantuck, which means "water that flows both ways."

"Taxi! TAXI!" Dad yells.
"Grand Central, please," I say.
Through the windows, the city
sparkles in the night.
Dad and I agree there's just
one thing better than taking a
walk in New York—and that's
riding a cab back!

The only way
you can catch
a New York cab
is if you hail it.

NAILS

Yankees

MAMMA'S PIZZA

203

SHO

不禮品
大酒求

24 HR PARK →

DRUG STORE

TAXI

TAXI TAXI

TAXI

TAXI

More than 12,000 licensed cabs work in NYC, and each one's sunshine yellow!

SWIFT COMPLETION OF THEIR APPOINTED ROUNDS

The New York
General Post Office
is open 24 hours a day,
seven days a week.

At the lights, the driver
shows me one last thing.
"That's the James A. Farley Building," he says.
"It has the General Post Office inside."
The writing carved around the top says,

"NEITHER SNOW, NOR RAIN, NOR HEAT,
NOR GLOOM OF NIGHT STAYS THESE
COURIERS FROM THE SWIFT COMPLETION
OF THEIR APPOINTED ROUNDS."

"What does it mean?" I ask.
"It's a promise that they'll do everything they can
to get your mail to you," Dad says.

So when we reach the station,
I write one of our postcards
and drop it in the mailbox. . . .

GRAND CENTRAL
TERMINAL

TAXI

U.S. MAIL

POSTCARD

Dear friend,
I hope one day
you'll come for
a walk in
New York, too.

x x x x

To you!

USA

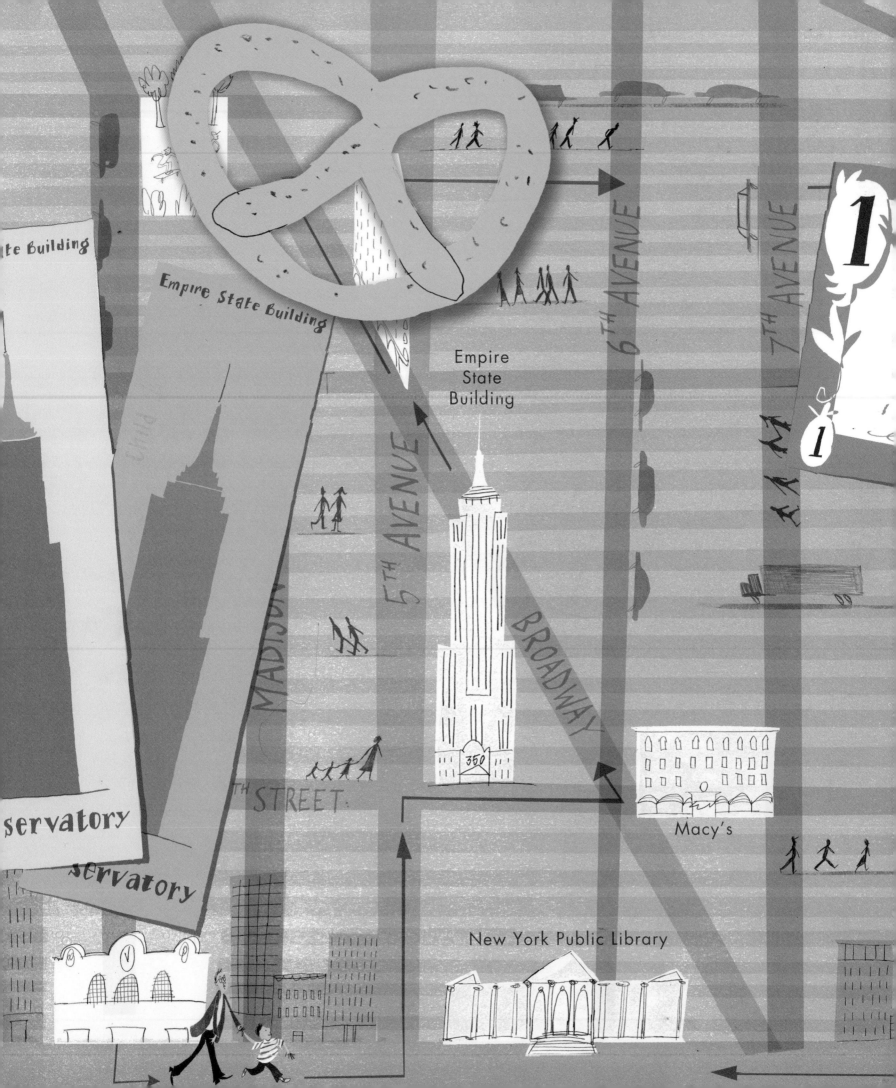